A sheep sat in
the sunshine.
"I am hot," said
the sheep.

1

"It must be fun to be
a fish," said the sheep.

"I shall jump in," said
the sheep.
"It will be fun to swim
and splash."

A fish came up to
the sheep.
The sheep stuck his
nose in.

"I see a rock," said
the sheep.
"That is not a rock,"
said the fish.
"It is a clam in
his shell."

5

"I see a cat," said
the sheep.
"She is not a cat," said
the fish.
"She is a catfish."

"I see a bug," said
the sheep.
"That is not a bug,"
said the fish.
"It is a shrimp."

"I see a big bug," said
the sheep.
"That is a crab," said
the fish.
"Look out!"

The sheep had to
shake the crab.
The crab let go
of his nose.

"I see grass," said
the sheep.
"That is not grass,"
said the fish.
"It is seaweed."

The sheep ate
the seaweed.
"That tastes bad,"
said the sheep.
"I do not like seaweed."

"I see a ship," said
the sheep.
"That is not a ship,"
said the fish.
"It is a sailboat."

"I must rush back to shore," said the sheep. "It is deep here. These waves scare me."

The sheep sat in the
shade of a tree.
"I am glad to be
back on land,"
said the sheep.

"Jump in," said
the fish.
"We can swim
and splash."

"No," said the sheep.
"I am glad to eat
real grass.
And I am so glad I am
a sheep."